moda All-Stars

cakewalk

A Carnival of Quilts That Begin with 10" Layer Cake Squares

Compiled by **Lissa Alexander**

Martingale®
Create with Confidence

Moda All-Stars
Cakewalk:
A Carnival of Quilts That Begin with 10" Layer Cake Squares
© 2020 by Martingale & Company®

Martingale®
19021 120th Ave. NE, Ste. 102
Bothell, WA 98011-9511 USA
ShopMartingale.com

Printed in Hong Kong
25 24 23 22 21 20   8 7 6 5 4 3 2 1

Library of Congress Cataloging-in-Publication Data
is available upon request.

ISBN: 978-1-68356-093-7

MISSION STATEMENT

We empower makers who use fabric and yarn to make life more enjoyable.

CREDITS

PUBLISHER AND
CHIEF VISIONARY OFFICER
Jennifer Erbe Keltner

CONTENT DIRECTOR
Karen Costello Soltys

MANAGING EDITOR
Tina Cook

ACQUISITIONS AND
DEVELOPMENT EDITOR
Laurie Baker

TECHNICAL WRITER
Elizabeth Beese

TECHNICAL EDITOR
Nancy Mahoney

COPY EDITOR
Durby Peterson

DESIGN MANAGER
Adrienne Smitke

PRODUCTION MANAGER
Regina Girard

COVER AND
BOOK DESIGNER
Kathy Kotomaimoce

PHOTOGRAPHERS
Adam Albright
Brent Kane

ILLUSTRATOR
Sandy Loi

SPECIAL THANKS

Photography for this book was taken at the homes of:
Lianne Anderson in Arlington, Washington
Karen Burns in Carnation, Washington
Bree Larson in Everett, Washington
Julie Smiley in Des Moines, Iowa
Libby Warnken in Ankeny, Iowa

contents

— ★ —

introduction

★

(Cue the cakewalk music and circle around.) What happens when you combine the joy of quilting with the ease of a Layer Cake (forty-two 10" squares)? Sweet success that's so much fun, that's what! And that's exactly what *Cakewalk* is all about—13 piece-of-cake quilt patterns that are simple to sew from fabrics that are a breeze to assort because you begin with precut 10" squares in varying prints.

The Moda All-Stars represent many of the talented designers who create Moda fabric lines. Do you have a favorite? Lisa Bongean, Corey Yoder, Me and My Sister, American Jane, Kansas Troubles Quilters, Sherri McConnell, Minick & Simpson, Kathy Schmitz, Brenda Riddle, Linzee McCray, Zen Chic, Deb Strain, and Betsy Chutchian—who can choose just one, right? Good news, you don't have to! We asked them *all* to begin with a Layer Cake (or two) from their own collections and add background prints as necessary. The results are delightful! Choose from wall hangings, throws, table toppers, and more (even a picnic blanket).

As with every Moda All-Stars book, your purchase paves the way for good because royalties for this book will be donated as a charitable contribution to Feed the Children (feedthechildren.org). Every dollar donated to this organization provides $7 worth of food and essentials to fight childhood hunger in the U.S. and around the world. Now that's a cause worth fighting for that together we can overcome!

Just like at the school carnival when you were a kid, choose your favorite spot in the book to begin. Our guess is that you'll find not just one, but a number of patterns to add to your "must-make" list. Every one is a winner! *(Cue the cakewalk music.)* Let's get this party started.

~Lissa Alexander

homey

By COREY YODER

What a fun riff on a classic Log Cabin block! Skip sorting scraps and create a scrappy-looking quilt by mixing and matching two Layer Cakes. All you need are 80 oh-so-easy blocks to make a borderless throw you'll want to wrap up in right away.

FINISHED QUILT	FINISHED BLOCK
60½" × 75½"	7½" × 7½"

materials

Yardage is based on 42"-wide fabric.

80 squares, 10" × 10", of assorted prints
for blocks*
⅝ yard of gray stripe for binding
4⅝ yards of fabric for backing
67" × 82" piece of batting

*A Moda Fabrics Layer Cake contains
42 squares, 10" × 10".*

cutting

All measurements include ¼"-wide seam allowances. Divide the 10" squares into 2 stacks of 40 squares each. Label 1 stack as A squares and the other stack as B squares. Refer to the cutting diagrams on page 9 to cut each stack of squares.

From *each* of the 40 A squares, cut:
2 rectangles, 2" × 6½" (80 total)
2 rectangles, 2" × 5" (80 total)
2 rectangles, 2" × 3½" (80 total)
2 squares, 2" × 2" (80 total)

Continued on page 9

By **COREY YODER**; quilted by **DAVID HURD**

Continued from page 7

From *each* of the 40 B squares, cut:

2 rectangles, 2" × 8" (80 total)
2 rectangles, 2" × 6½" (80 total)
2 rectangles, 2" × 5" (80 total)
2 rectangles, 2" × 3½" (80 total)
2 squares, 2" × 2" (80 total)

From the gray stripe, cut:

7 strips, 2½" × 42"

10"	
2" × 6½"	2" × 3½"
2" × 6½"	2" × 3½"
2" × 5"	2" × 2"
2" × 5"	2" × 2"

Cutting for A squares

10"	
2" × 8"	2" × 2"
2" × 8"	2" × 2"
2" × 6½"	2" × 3½"
2" × 6½"	2" × 3½"
2" × 5"	2" × 5"

Cutting for B squares

making the blocks

Press all seam allowances as indicated by the arrows.

1 Join two print 2" squares to make a two-patch unit. Make 80 units measuring 2" × 3½", including seam allowances.

Make 80 units,
2" × 3½".

2 Sew a print 2" × 3½" rectangle to the top of a two-patch unit from step 1. Sew a different print 2" × 3½" rectangle to the left edge. Sew a different print 2" × 5" rectangle to the bottom edge to make a unit. Make 80 units measuring 5" square, including seam allowances.

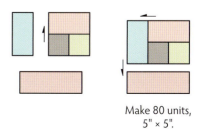

Make 80 units,
5" × 5".

3 Working in a counterclockwise direction, sew a print 2" × 5" rectangle to the right edge of a unit from step 2. Sew print 2" × 6½" rectangles to the top and left edges. Sew a print 2" × 8" rectangle to the bottom edge to make a block. Make 80 blocks measuring 8" square, including seam allowances.

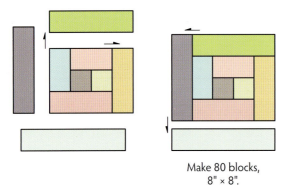

Make 80 blocks,
8" × 8".

PLANNED APPROACH?

Try playing with fabric placement. When choosing your A and B squares, select light-colored fabrics for A and dark-colored fabrics for B. This will allow you to create Log Cabin blocks that are dark on one half of the block and light on the other half.

assembling the quilt top

Lay out the blocks in 10 rows of eight blocks each, rotating the blocks in each row and from row to row as shown in the quilt assembly diagram. Sew the blocks into rows. Join the rows to complete the quilt top. The quilt top should measure 60½" × 75½".

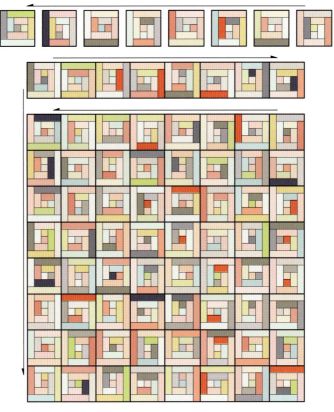

Quilt assembly

finishing the quilt

Find free, detailed finishing instructions online at ShopMartingale.com/HowtoQuilt.

1 Prepare the quilt backing so it's about 6" larger in both directions than the quilt top.

2 Layer the backing, batting, and quilt top. Baste the layers together.

3 Hand or machine quilt as desired. The quilt shown is machine quilted with an allover diamond spiral design.

4 Use the gray stripe 2½"-wide strips to make binding. Attach the binding to the quilt.

corey
YODER

★

Here's a tip to make sewing my quilt a piece of cake: Starting with two Layer Cakes means the cutting on this one is going to be a cinch.

If I were in charge of the music for the carnival cakewalk, the song I'd play most is: something upbeat!

When it comes to notions and tools, this one takes the cake for me: I love the Stripology rulers for cutting lots of squares and rectangles quickly.

Any way you slice it, the best thing about a Layer Cake is: They're so versatile—my favorite precut.

Take a number. When I'm buying fabric to use along with a Layer Cake: I most often get a solid—probably Bella Solid in 9900-200, 9900-170, or 9900-171 (Off White, Etchings Slate, and Etchings Charcoal).

Food for thought: What's one thing you wish more quilters would do? Be unafraid to try new things. Sometimes things don't work out on the first try, but they might on the second or third!

What's the frosting on the cake for you in the quiltmaking process? Choosing and buying fabric—the buying part is always especially fun. I also enjoy visiting new quilt shops and hitting a good restaurant on the way there . . . and on the way home.

When slicing up a Layer Cake, my go-to ruler and rotary cutter are: my Creative Grids 6½" × 18½" ruler and OLFA 60 mm cutter.

There's always room for cake. True confessions—how many Layer Cakes are in your stash now? Hmm . . . I plead the fifth.

Eat dessert first. What's your favorite treat before beginning a new project? I like to cut all the pieces and then decide what podcast I'll be listening to, and maybe I'll grab a tea or coffee.

My all-time favorite cake is: My mom makes the yummiest oatmeal cake—it's sugary deliciousness.

CorianderQuilts.com

explore
by DEB STRAIN

Inspired by a Layer Cake with a nature theme, Deb created Star blocks that invite us to venture into the trees. A flying-geese border completes the design and continues the feeling of getting back to nature. One word to describe Explore is *fun!*

FINISHED QUILT	FINISHED BLOCK
40½" × 40½"	8" × 8"

materials

Yardage is based on 42"-wide fabric.

8 squares, 10" × 10", for blocks (2 *each* of red, blue, gold, and green prints)*

5 squares, 10" × 10", of tan or cream print for blocks and border (collectively referred to as "cream")*

12 squares, 10" × 10", of assorted prints for border*

⅞ yard of ivory print for blocks

1 yard of green plaid for border and binding

2½ yards of fabric for backing

45" × 45" piece of batting

A Moda Fabrics Layer Cake contains 42 squares, 10"×10".

cutting

All measurements include ¼"-wide seam allowances. Refer to the cutting diagram on page 15 to cut the red, blue, gold, and green 10" squares.

From *each* of the 8 red, blue, gold, and green print squares, cut:
8 squares, 2½" × 2½" (64 total)
1 rectangle, 4¼" × 4½" (8 total)
1 square, 1¼" × 1¼" (8 total)

From *each* of the 5 cream print squares, cut:
4 squares, 4½" × 4½" (20 total)

From the 12 assorted print squares, cut a *total* of:
16 squares, 4½" × 4½"
64 rectangles, 2½" × 4½"

Continued on page 15

By **DEB STRAIN;** pieced by **NATALIE CRABTREE;**
quilted by **STEPHANIE CRABTREE**

Continued from page 13

From the ivory print, cut:

2 strips, 3¼" × 42"; crosscut into 16 rectangles, 3¼" × 4½"

7 strips, 2½" × 42"; crosscut into:
32 rectangles, 2½" × 4½"
32 squares, 2½" × 2½"

1 strip, 1¼" × 42"; crosscut into 16 rectangles, 1¼" × 2¼"

From the green plaid, cut:

13 strips, 2½" × 42"; crosscut *8 of the strips* into 128 squares, 2½" × 2½"

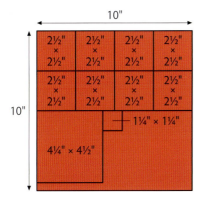

Cutting for red, blue, gold, and green squares

making the tree units

Press all seam allowances as indicated by the arrows.

1 Fold each red, blue, gold, and green 4¼" × 4½" rectangle in half lengthwise; press and unfold. Align a ruler with the top of the pressed crease and the lower-left corner of the rectangle; trim. Repeat to trim the right half of the rectangle in the same way. Cut eight triangles.

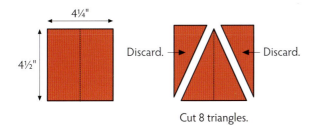

Cut 8 triangles.

2 On an ivory print 3¼" × 4½" rectangle, mark a point 1" from the upper-left corner. Align a ruler with the mark and the lower-right corner of the rectangle; trim. Cut eight background pieces.

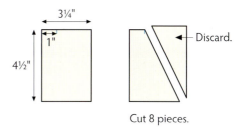

Cut 8 pieces.

3 On an ivory print 3¼" × 4½" rectangle, mark a point 1" from the upper-right corner. Align a ruler with the mark and the lower-left corner of the rectangle; trim. Cut eight reversed background pieces.

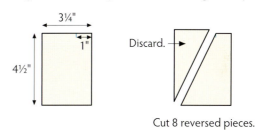

Cut 8 reversed pieces.

4 Sew ivory background and reversed background pieces to a triangle from step 1 to make a tree-top unit. Trim the unit to 3¾" × 4½", including seam allowances, being sure to leave a ¼" seam allowance beyond the top of the triangle. Make eight units.

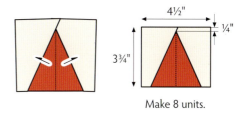

Make 8 units.

5 Join two ivory 1¼" × 2¼" rectangles and one red, blue, gold, or green 1¼" square. Trim the ends to make a trunk unit measuring 1¼" × 4½", including seam allowances. Make eight units.

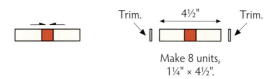

Make 8 units,
1¼" × 4½".

together. Sew on the marked line. Trim the excess corner fabric ¼" from the stitched line. Place a marked square on the opposite end of the ivory rectangle. Sew and trim as before to make a flying-geese unit measuring 2½" × 4½", including seam allowances. Make 32 units.

Make 32 units,
2½" × 4½".

2 Matching the red, blue, gold, or green print, lay out four flying-geese units, one tree unit, and four ivory 2½" squares in three rows. Sew the pieces into rows. Join the rows to make a Star block measuring 8½" square, including seam allowances. Make eight blocks.

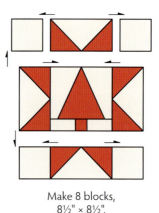

Make 8 blocks,
8½" × 8½".

making the four patch blocks

1 Set aside four matching cream 4½" squares for the border corners.

2 Lay out two cream 4½" squares and two print 4½" squares in two rows of two. Sew the pieces into rows. Join the rows to make a Four

6 Matching the red, blue, gold, or green print, sew a tree-top unit to a trunk unit to make a tree unit measuring 4½" square, including seam allowances. Make eight units.

Make 8 tree units,
4½" × 4½".

making the star blocks

1 Draw a diagonal line from corner to corner on the wrong side of each red, blue, gold, and green 2½" square. Place a marked square on one end of an ivory 2½" × 4½" rectangle, right sides

Patch block measuring 8½" square, including seam allowances. Make eight blocks.

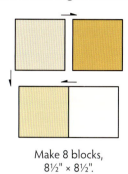

Make 8 blocks,
8½" × 8½".

making the flying-geese border

1 Draw a diagonal line from corner to corner on the wrong side of each green plaid square. Referring to step 1 of "Making the Star Blocks" on page 16, use two marked squares and one print 2½" × 4½" rectangle to make a flying-geese unit measuring 2½" × 4½", including seam allowances. Make 64 units.

Make 64 units,
2½" × 4½".

2 Noting the orientation of the units, join 16 flying-geese units to make a side border measuring 4½" × 32½", including seam allowances. Make two. Make two top/bottom borders in the same manner, adding a reserved cream square to each end. The top/bottom borders should measure 4½" × 40½", including seam allowances.

Side border.
Make 2 borders, 4½" × 32½".

Top/bottom border.
Make 2 borders, 4½" × 40½".

deb
STRAIN

★

If I were in charge of the music for the carnival cakewalk, the song I'd play most is: "Dancin' on the Ceiling" by Lionel Richie or "Happy" by Pharrell Williams. They're both perfect to get me moving, especially when I'm cleaning the house or working on a deadline!

When it comes to notions and tools, this one takes the cake for me: Because I am an amateur sewist, my favorite tool is the seam ripper. It's always close by and used often when I'm sewing!

Any way you slice it, the best thing about a Layer Cake is: I can see all of the colors and patterns from the entire fabric group together and there's so much of each one. Layer Cakes are my favorite precut!

Food for thought: What's one thing you wish more quilters would do? I wish they'd share photos of their finished projects using my fabrics! I love to see what they create using the patterns and colors that I have so lovingly designed.

There's always room for cake. True confessions— how many Layer Cakes are in your stash now? At least one from every fabric line that I've designed since Moda started making Layer Cakes. That's more than 40!

Eat dessert first. What's your favorite treat before beginning a new project? I try to clean off a space (big challenge right there!) where I can spread out all my fabric. I turn on my favorite music, relax, and enjoy mixing and matching the patterns and colors.

My all-time favorite cake is: Carrot cake! There's a place about a mile away from my home that sells a wonderful carrot cake by the slice. Sometimes I reward myself by walking there and eating the entire piece on the way home.

Instagram: @debstrain

assembling the quilt top

1 Lay out the Star blocks and Four Patch blocks in four rows of four blocks each, alternating them as shown in the quilt assembly diagram. Sew the blocks into rows. Join the rows to make a quilt center measuring 32½" square, including seam allowances.

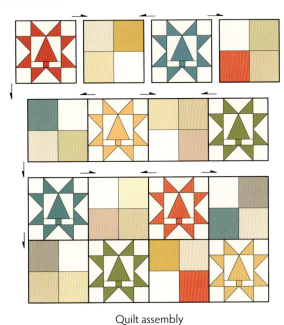

Quilt assembly

2 Sew the side border strips to opposite sides of the quilt center. Add the top/bottom border strips to the remaining sides to complete the quilt top. The quilt top should measure 40½" square.

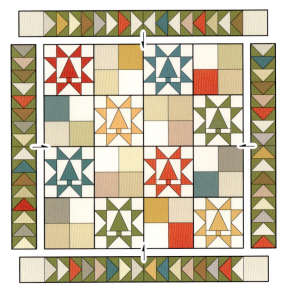

Adding the border

finishing the quilt

Find free, detailed finishing instructions online at ShopMartingale.com/HowtoQuilt.

1 Prepare the quilt backing so it's about 4" larger in both directions than the quilt top.

2 Layer the backing, batting, and quilt top. Baste the layers together.

3 Hand or machine quilt as desired. The quilt shown is machine quilted with a leaf-and-acorn design.

4 Use the remaining green plaid 2½"-wide strips to make binding. Attach the binding to the quilt.

variable star

By LINZEE KULL McCRAY and PAM EHRHARDT

In nature, a variable star is one whose brightness seems to flicker. In the Variable Star quilt, the combination of light and dark fabrics makes each star unique. The simple-to-sew pattern employs clever cutting to make quick work of creating a starry field. It's the perfect quilt to snuggle under while scanning the skies in your own backyard.

FINISHED QUILT	FINISHED BLOCK
60½" × 75½"	7½" × 7½"

materials

Yardage is based on 42"-wide fabric.

40 squares, 10" × 10", of assorted prints for blocks*
3⅛ yards of white solid for blocks
⅝ yard of multicolored print for binding
4⅝ yards of fabric for backing
67" × 82" piece of batting

A Moda Fabrics Layer Cake contains 42 squares, 10" × 10".

cutting

All measurements include ¼"-wide seam allowances.

From the white solid, cut:
10 strips, 10" × 42"; crosscut into 40 squares, 10" × 10"

From the multicolored print, cut:
8 strips, 2½" × 42"

making the blocks

Press all seam allowances as indicated by the arrows.

1 Mark a diagonal line from corner to corner on the wrong side of each white solid 10" square. Layer a marked square on a print 10" square, right sides together. Sew ¼" from both sides of the drawn line. Cut the unit apart on the marked line to make

two half-square-triangle units. Trim the units to 9" square, including seam allowances. Make 80 units.

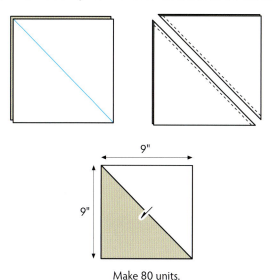

Make 80 units.

2 Place a half-square-triangle unit on the cutting mat as shown and cut it into three strips measuring 3" × 9", including seam allowances.

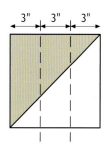
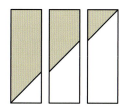

Cut half-square-triangle unit into three 3" × 9" strips.

3 Rotate the strips from step 2 horizontally and rearrange them as shown. The position of the strips is very important for the next cut. Line up the edges of the three strips with the horizontal and vertical lines of the cutting mat.

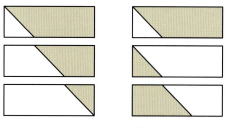

Rearrange strips.

4 Make a vertical cut 3" from the left edge through all three strips. On the top two strips, make a second cut, 5½" from the first cut. On the bottom strip only, make a second cut that is 3" from the first cut.

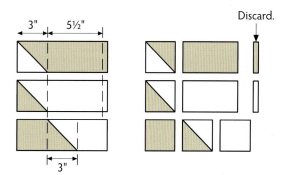

5 Rearrange the pieces in three rows as shown. Sew the pieces into rows. Join the rows to make a block measuring 8" square, including seam allowances. Make a total of 80 blocks.

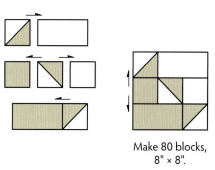

Make 80 blocks, 8" × 8".

By LINZEE McCRAY and PAM EHRHARDT

Cakewalk

assembling the quilt top

Lay out the blocks in 10 rows of eight blocks each, rotating the blocks in each row and from row to row to form stars as shown in the quilt assembly diagram. Sew the blocks into rows. Join the rows to complete the quilt top. The quilt top should measure 60½" × 75½".

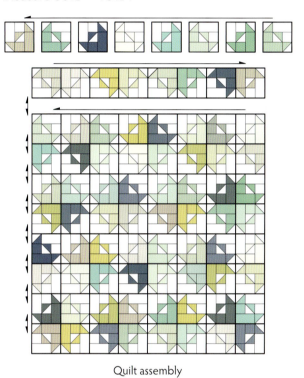

Quilt assembly

finishing the quilt

Find free, detailed finishing instructions online at ShopMartingale.com/HowtoQuilt.

1 Prepare the quilt backing so it's about 6" larger in both directions than the quilt top.

2 Layer the backing, batting, and quilt top. Baste the layers together.

3 Hand or machine quilt as desired. The quilt shown is machine quilted with an allover paisley design.

4 Use the multicolored 2½"-wide strips to make binding. Attach the binding to the quilt.

Here's a tip to make sewing my quilt a piece of cake: Pay close attention to the pressing directions to prevent a lump where the seams intersect.

If I were in charge of the music for the carnival cakewalk, the song I'd play most is: "Walkin' After Midnight" by Patsy Cline.

When it comes to notions and tools, this one takes the cake for me: Clover Wonder Clips (the mini ones). I use them when binding quilts, making a bag with lots of layers, or stitching something that doesn't take well to pins, like oilcloth.

Any way you slice it, the best thing about Layer Cakes is: The versatility—you can cut one up in so many ways (mini charms or charm packs, anyone?) or use them just as they are.

Food for thought: What's one thing you wish more quilters would do? As a feed-sack fanatic, I'm a fan of making do. I hope quilters won't worry so much if everything doesn't match exactly or if they run out of a particular fabric—the lack of consistency in antique quilts makes them charming, and that'll make our quilts charming to future collectors too!

What's the frosting on the cake for you in the quiltmaking process? The beginning and the end. I love the excitement of planning a new quilt and I love binding it when it's done.

When slicing up a Layer Cake, my go-to ruler and rotary cutter are: After years of using the OLFA 45 mm rotary cutter, I discovered the OLFA 60 mm and I'm never going back! (Well, unless I need to cut something tiny.)

Eat dessert first. What's your favorite treat before beginning a new project? Planning to order take-out . . . hello, pizza!

What's your go-to batting between layers of your quilt top and backing? Wool batting—it's lightweight and comfortable in summer and winter.

linzeekullmccray.com

all squared up

by SHERRI L. McCONNELL

Have you been hoarding Layer Cakes? Here's a perfectly easy design to use at least one stack of squares! Just pair up the pieces from two contrasting prints and sew. Add solid ivory sashing and a pretty floral border, and it all adds up to one delectable quilt.

FINISHED QUILT	FINISHED BLOCK
50½" × 57½"	6" × 6"

materials

Yardage is based on 42"-wide fabric.

42 squares, 10" × 10", of assorted prints for blocks*
⅞ yard of ivory solid for sashing and inner border
⅝ yard of coral print for sashing squares and binding
¾ yard of aqua floral for outer border
3¼ yards of fabric for backing
57" × 64" piece of batting

A Moda Fabrics Layer Cake contains 42 squares, 10" × 10".

cutting

All measurements include ¼"-wide seam allowances.

From *each* of the 42 assorted print squares, cut:
1 square, 4¾" × 4¾" (42 total)
2 squares, 4⅜" × 4⅜" (84 total); cut the squares in half diagonally to yield 4 triangles (168 total)

From the ivory solid, cut:
17 strips, 1½" × 42"; crosscut *12 of the strips* into 71 rectangles, 1½" × 6½"

From the coral print, cut:
6 strips, 2½" × 42"
2 strips, 1½" × 42"; crosscut into 30 squares, 1½" × 1½"

From the aqua floral, cut:
6 strips, 4" × 42"

25

making the blocks

Press all seam allowances as indicated by the arrows.

Select four triangles from one print and a 4¾" square from a second print. Center and sew triangles to opposite edges of the square. Center and sew triangles to the remaining edges of the square to make a block. Trim the block to 6½" square, making sure to leave ¼" beyond the points for seam allowances. Make 42 blocks.

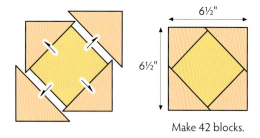

Make 42 blocks.

assembling the quilt top

1 Join six blocks and five ivory rectangles to make a block row. Make seven rows measuring 6½" × 41½", including seam allowances.

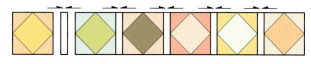

Make 7 rows,
6½" × 41½".

2 Join six ivory rectangles and five coral squares to make a sashing row. Make six rows measuring 1½" × 41½", including seam allowances.

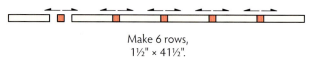

Make 6 rows,
1½" × 41½".

3 Lay out the block rows and sashing rows, alternating them as shown in the quilt assembly diagram. Join the rows to make a quilt-top center measuring 41½" × 48½", including seam allowances.

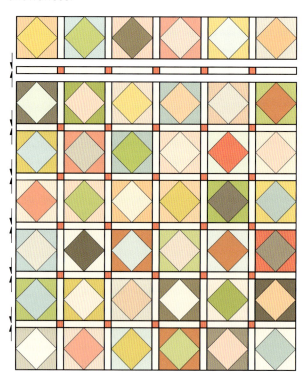

Quilt assembly

4 Join the remaining ivory 1½" × 42" strips end to end to make a long strip. From the pieced strip, cut two 48½"-long strips and two 43½"-long strips. Sew the longer strips to opposite sides of the quilt top. Sew the shorter strips to the top and bottom. The quilt top should measure 43½" × 50½", including seam allowances.

By SHERRI McCONNELL; quilted by MARION BOTT

sherri
McCONNELL

Here's a tip to make sewing my quilt a piece of cake: Pair the prints for all the blocks *before* you begin to sew.

If I were in charge of the music for the carnival cakewalk, the song I'd play most is: "Perfect" by Ed Sheeran.

When it comes to notions and tools, this one takes the cake for me: I love the Mini Simple Folded Corners Ruler for fast and accurate sewing.

Any way you slice it, the best thing about Layer Cakes is: You can always make a simple patchwork throw with all 42 squares!

Take a number. When I'm buying fabric to use along with a Layer Cake: I usually buy a couple of yards of background and two different one-yard pieces for the border and binding.

Food for thought: What's one thing you wish more quilters would do? Really enjoy the process and not worry so much about perfection.

What's the frosting on the cake for you in the quiltmaking process? I love binding and then enjoying the finished quilt.

When slicing up a Layer Cake, my go-to ruler and rotary cutter are: an 8½" × 12" ruler with an OLFA Splash Rotary Cutter. I love the new navy color!

There's always room for cake. True confessions—how many Layer Cakes are in your stash now? About 12.

Eat dessert first. What's your favorite treat before beginning a new project? I clean up my work table and sewing room and make sure the menu is planned so I can devote all of my time to sewing.

What's your go-to batting between layers of your quilt top and backing? Warm & White!

My all-time favorite cake is: chocolate cake with chocolate frosting!

AQuiltingLife.com

5 Join the aqua strips end to end to make a long strip. From the pieced strip, cut four 50½"-long strips. Sew strips to opposite sides of the quilt top. Sew the remaining strips to the top and bottom to complete the quilt top. The quilt top should measure 50½" × 57½".

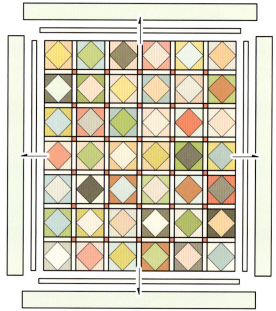

Adding borders

finishing the quilt

Find free, detailed finishing instructions online at ShopMartingale.com/HowtoQuilt.

1 Prepare the quilt backing so it's about 6" larger in both directions than the quilt top.

2 Layer the backing, batting, and quilt top. Baste the layers together.

3 Hand or machine quilt as desired. The quilt shown is machine quilted with an allover flower-and-circle design.

4 Use the coral 2½"-wide strips to make binding. Attach the binding to the quilt.

county fair

by BRENDA RIDDLE

You might not be seeing stars when you first glance at this sweet quilt, but watching the stars come out is part of the fun! Careful fabric placement and a Layer Cake of soft florals is the trick to the stars' subtle look. The light background creates a visual puzzle, making it difficult to distinguish the blocks from the sashing.

FINISHED QUILT	FINISHED BLOCK
44½" × 44½"	8" × 8"

materials

Yardage is based on 42"-wide fabric.

32 squares, 10" × 10", for blocks and sashing
    (8 *each* of pink, aqua, taupe, and ivory prints)*
⅝ yard *each* of 2 different light dots for blocks
    and sashing
⅝ yard of ivory solid for sashing
½ yard of sea-foam green print for binding
2⅞ yards of fabric for backing
51" × 51" piece of batting

*A Moda Fabrics Layer Cake contains
42 squares, 10" × 10".

cutting

*All measurements include ¼"-wide seam allowances.
Separate the pink, aqua, and taupe print 10" squares
from the ivory print 10" squares.*

From *each* of the 24 pink, aqua, and taupe print squares, cut:
1 rectangle, 4½" × 8½" (24 total)
From the scraps of pink, aqua, and taupe prints, cut a *total* of:
100 squares, 2½" × 2½"
From the 8 ivory print squares, cut:
5 squares, 8½" × 8½"
9 squares, 4½" × 4½"
From the light dots, cut a *total* of:
11 squares, 8½" × 8½"
From the ivory solid, cut:
7 strips, 2½" × 42"; crosscut into 96 squares,
    2½" × 2½"
From the sea-foam green print, cut:
5 strips, 2½" × 42"

making the blocks and sashing units

Press all seam allowances as indicated by the arrows.

1 Draw a diagonal line from corner to corner on the wrong side of each pink, aqua, and taupe 2½" square. Place a marked square on each corner of an ivory or light dot 8½" square, right sides together. Sew on the marked lines. Trim the excess corner fabric ¼" from the stitched lines. Make 16 blocks, 8½" square.

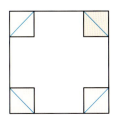 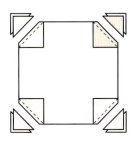

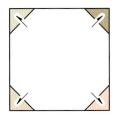

Make 16 blocks,
8½" × 8½".

2 Place marked squares from step 1 on opposite corners of an ivory print 4½" square, right sides together. Sew and trim as before. Sew marked squares to the two remaining corners. Trim and press to make a cornerstone unit. Make nine units measuring 4½" square, including seam allowances.

Make 9 units,
4½" × 4½".

3 Draw a diagonal line from corner to corner on the wrong side of the ivory solid squares. Repeat step 2 to sew marked squares on a pink, aqua, or taupe rectangle to make a sashing unit. Make 24 units measuring 4½" × 8½", including seam allowances.

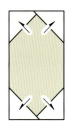

Make 24 units,
4½" × 8½".

assembling the quilt top

1 Join four blocks and three sashing units to make a block row. Make four rows measuring 8½" × 44½", including seam allowances.

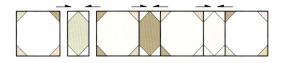

Make 4 rows,
8½" × 44½".

By BRENDA RIDDLE

Cakewalk

2 Join four sashing units and three cornerstone units to make a sashing row. Make three rows measuring 4½" × 44½", including seam allowances.

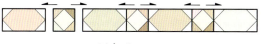

Make 3 rows,
4½" × 44½".

3 Join the block rows and sashing rows to complete a quilt top measuring 44½" square.

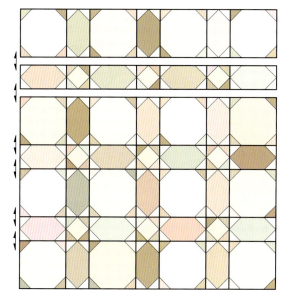

Quilt assembly

finishing the quilt

Find free, detailed finishing instructions online at ShopMartingale.com/HowtoQuilt.

1 Prepare the quilt backing so it's about 6" larger in both directions than the quilt top.

2 Layer the backing, batting, and quilt top. Baste the layers together.

3 Hand or machine quilt as desired. The quilt shown is machine quilted with an allover floral design.

4 Use the sea-foam green 2½"-wide strips to make binding. Attach the binding to the quilt.

brenda
RIDDLE

Here's a tip to make sewing my quilt a piece of cake: When pressing triangles open, take your time. They'll lay down so much better if you press slowly.

If I were in charge of the music for the carnival cakewalk, the song I'd play most is: "Can't Stop the Feeling" by Justin Timberlake. (How can you not love a lyric like "I got that sunshine in my pocket"?)

When it comes to notions and tools, this one takes the cake for me: Colonial ThimblePads. They're little suede dots with adhesive that work in the place of a thimble, making hand stitching such a pleasure.

Any way you slice it, the best thing about Layer Cakes is: That you get one (or more!) of every print in a collection in a great size. Not too small, not too big. They're just right!

Take a number. When I'm buying fabric to use along with a Layer Cake: I choose Bella Solid Off White. It's my go-to soft white . . . and I ~~hoard~~ have bolts of it always at the ready.

Food for thought: What's one thing you wish more quilters would do? Know that unless they're making a quilt to be judged, there aren't any quilt police. Quilts don't need to be perfectly pieced to be perfect.

What's the frosting on the cake for you in the quiltmaking process? It's a tie between hand binding (I love that process!) and when I first wash a quilt and take it out of the dryer, because it has an instant vintage and well-loved look.

When slicing up a Layer Cake, my go-to ruler and rotary cutter are: The Creative Grids 6" × 24" ruler for cutting strips and the 4½" × 12" ruler for subcutting. And my pink OLFA 45 mm rotary cutter.

Eat dessert first. What's your favorite treat before beginning a new project? A fresh cup of coffee and making sure I have several bobbins wound so I (hopefully) won't have to wind any along the way.

My all-time favorite cake is: coffee cake.

BrendaRiddleDesigns.com

orange crush

By LAURIE SIMPSON

Contrast is the key to getting colorful patchwork to pop off the solid orange background. Choose your favorite Layer Cake and do a little strip piecing to make scrappy-looking blocks. Set them on point and finish a fabulous quilt in no time!

FINISHED QUILT	FINISHED BLOCK
78¼" × 78¼"	8" × 8"

materials

Yardage is based on 42"-wide fabric.

36 squares, 10" × 10", of assorted prints for blocks*

1⅛ yards of white with black dots (referred to as "white polka dot") for blocks

4 yards of orange solid for setting squares, setting triangles, and border

¾ yard of blue plaid for binding

7¼ yards of fabric for backing

87" × 87" piece of batting

A Moda Fabrics Layer Cake contains 42 squares, 10"×10".

cutting

All measurements include ¼"-wide seam allowances. When cutting the 1½"×10" strips from the assorted prints, try not to use any prints that have a white background. You can use prints with a white background for the 4½" squares.

From *each* of the 36 assorted print squares, cut:

2 squares, 4½" × 4½" (72 total)

3 strips, 1½" × 10" (108 total; 12 are extra)

From the white polka dot, cut:

24 strips, 1½" × 42"; crosscut into 96 strips, 1½" × 10"

From the orange solid, cut:

2 strips, 12⅝" × 42"; crosscut into:

    5 squares, 12⅝" × 12⅝"; cut the squares into quarters diagonally to yield 20 side triangles

    2 squares, 6⅝" × 6⅝"; cut the squares in half diagonally to yield 4 corner triangles

7 strips, 8½" × 42"; crosscut into 25 squares, 8½" × 8½"

8 strips, 5½" × 42"

From the blue plaid, cut:

Enough bias-cut strips, 2½" wide, to total 335"

2 Join two units to make a strip set. Make 48 strip sets measuring 4½" × 10", including seam allowances. Cut each strip set into six segments, 1½" × 4½" (288 total).

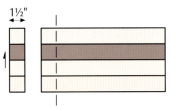

Make 48 strip sets, 4½" × 10".
Cut 288 segments, 1½" × 4½".

3 Join four segments to make a 16-patch unit, rotating every other segment as shown. Make 72 units measuring 4½" square, including seam allowances.

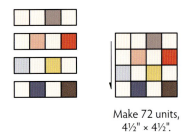

Make 72 units,
4½" × 4½".

4 Lay out two matching print 4½" squares and two 16-patch units in two rows of two. Sew the pieces into rows. Join the rows to make a block. Make 36 blocks measuring 8½" square, including seam allowances.

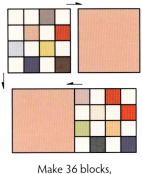

Make 36 blocks,
8½" × 8½".

making the blocks

Press all seam allowances as indicated by the arrows.

1 Join a print 1½" × 10" strip and a white polka dot 1½" × 10" strip to make a strip unit. Make 96 units measuring 2½" × 10", including seam allowances.

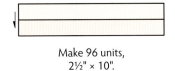

Make 96 units,
2½" × 10".

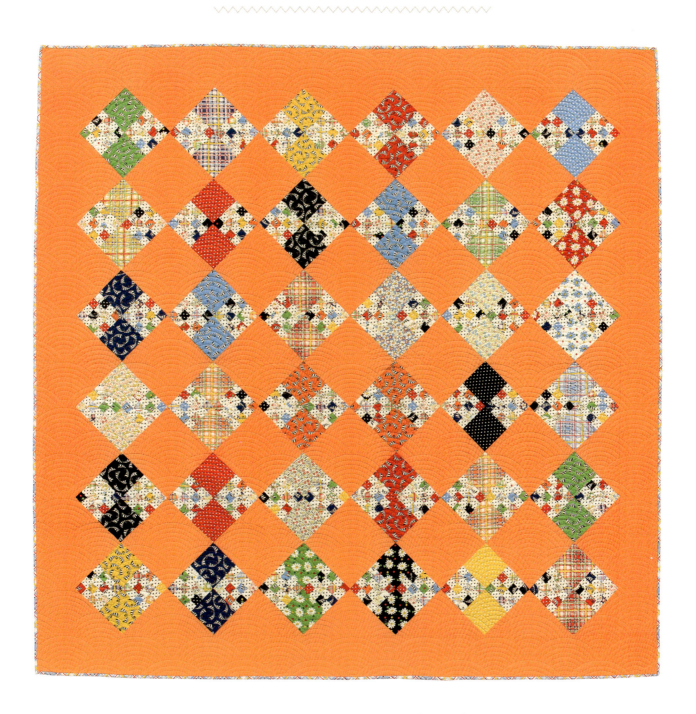

By LAURIE SIMPSON; quilted by MAGGI HONEYMAN

assembling the quilt top

1 Lay out the blocks, orange 8½" squares, and orange side and corner triangles in diagonal rows as shown in the quilt assembly diagram below. Sew the pieces into rows. Join the rows, adding the corner triangles last.

2 Trim and square up the quilt top, making sure to leave ¼" beyond the points of all blocks for seam allowances. The quilt top should measure 68¼" square, including seam allowances.

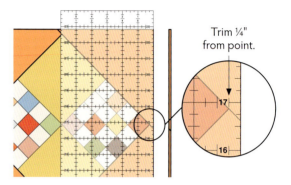

Trim ¼" from point.

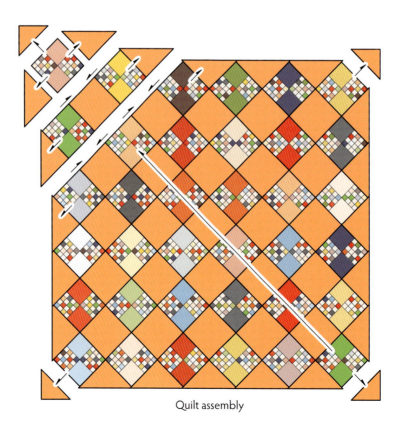

Quilt assembly

3 Join the orange 5½" × 42" strips end to end to make a long strip. From the pieced strip, cut two 68¼"-long strips and two 78¼"-long strips. Sew the shorter strips to opposite sides of the quilt top. Sew the longer strips to the top and bottom of the quilt top. The quilt top should measure 78¼" square.

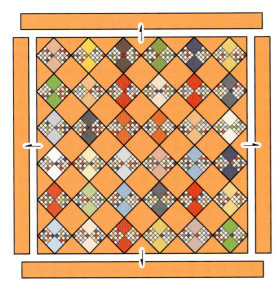

Adding the border

finishing the quilt

Find free, detailed finishing instructions online at ShopMartingale.com/HowtoQuilt.

1 Prepare the quilt backing so it's about 8" larger in both directions than the quilt top.

2 Layer the backing, batting, and quilt top. Baste the layers together.

3 Hand or machine quilt as desired. The quilt shown is machine quilted with an allover Baptist Fan design.

4 Use the blue plaid 2½"-wide bias strips to make binding. Attach the binding to the quilt.

laurie
SIMPSON

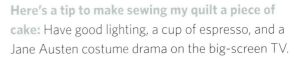

Here's a tip to make sewing my quilt a piece of cake: Have good lighting, a cup of espresso, and a Jane Austen costume drama on the big-screen TV.

If I were in charge of the music for the carnival cakewalk, the song I'd play most is: "I'm Gonna Be (500 Miles)" by the Proclaimers.

When it comes to notions and tools, this one takes the cake for me: Japanese thread snips. I keep them on the bed of my sewing machine to cut apart my chain stitching.

Take a number. When buying fabric to use along with a Layer Cake: I buy enough for the background of a queen-size quilt, somewhere between three and six yards of something wonderful.

Food for thought: What's one thing you wish more quilters would do? Give up on being perfect. It's not only overrated, it often gets in the way of creativity.

What's the frosting on the cake for you in the quiltmaking process? Handwork—it may be hand piecing, hand appliqué, or hand quilting.

When slicing up a Layer Cake, my go-to ruler and rotary cutter are: a 60 mm cutter and a 6" × 24" ruler, although I have every size of cutter and almost every ruler made!

There's always room for cake. True confessions— how many Layer Cakes are in your stash now? 18.

Eat dessert first. What's your favorite treat before beginning a new project? I clean off the cutting table, drafting table, and desktop, then put in a new rotary blade, and if I'm machine piecing, insert a new needle. And maybe a package of Starburst.

What is your go-to batting between quilt layers? Either 100% cotton or wool. I use Hobbs for machine quilting, wool for hand quilting with a small needle, and Quilters Dream for big-stitch hand quilting.

My all-time favorite cake is: yellow cake with chocolate frosting, two layers.

MinickandSimpson.blogspot.com

walk in the woods

By SANDY KLOP

The secret to making these traditional blocks begins with pairing up Layer Cake squares. Cut the 10" squares into smaller squares and rectangles, rearrange the pieces, and you're ready to sew! Lay out the setting squares in diagonal rows to create a terrific secondary design.

FINISHED QUILT	FINISHED BLOCK
68½" × 94"	8½" × 8½"

materials

Yardage is based on 42"-wide fabric.

44 squares, 10" × 10", of assorted prints for blocks*

⅓ yard *each* of green dot and aqua check for setting squares

⅝ yard *each* of red dot, white floral, red check, and yellow dot for setting squares

⅞ yard of blue chambray for setting squares

¾ yard of navy dot for binding

5¾ yards of fabric for backing

77" × 102" piece of batting

A Moda Fabrics Layer Cake contains 42 squares, 10"×10".

cutting

All measurements include ¼"-wide seam allowances. Refer to the cutting diagram below to cut the assorted print 10" squares.

From *each* of the 44 assorted print squares, cut:

1 square, 5" × 5" (44 total)

4 rectangles, 2½" × 5" (176 total)

4 squares, 2½" × 2½" (176 total)

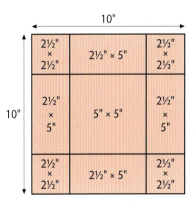

Cutting for 10" squares

From the green dot, cut:

1 strip, 9" × 42"; crosscut into 3 squares, 9" × 9"

From the aqua check, cut:

1 strip, 9" × 42"; crosscut into 4 squares, 9" × 9"

From the red dot, cut:

2 strips, 9" × 42"; crosscut into 5 squares, 9" × 9"

From the white floral, cut:

2 strips, 9" × 42"; crosscut into 7 squares, 9" × 9"

From the red check, cut:

2 strips, 9" × 42"; crosscut into 8 squares, 9" × 9"

Continued on page 43

By SANDY KLOP

Continued from page 41

From the yellow dot, cut:

2 strips, 9" × 42"; crosscut into 6 squares, 9" × 9"

From the blue chambray, cut:

3 strips, 9" × 42"; crosscut into 11 squares, 9" × 9"

From the navy dot, cut:

9 strips, 2½" × 42"

making the blocks

Press all seam allowances as indicated by the arrows.

1 Lay out the pieces from two different 10" squares in the same positions as you cut them. Swap the 2½" × 5" rectangles so that each arrangement contains pieces from both 10" squares.

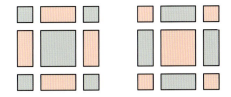

2 Sew the pieces into rows. Join the rows to make a block measuring 9" square, including seam allowances. Repeat to make a reversed block. Make 22 blocks and 22 reversed blocks (44 total).

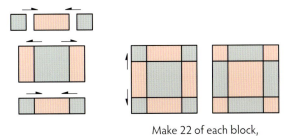

Make 22 of each block,
9" × 9".

assembling the quilt top

Lay out the blocks and the green dot, aqua check, red dot, white floral, red check, yellow dot, and blue chambray squares in 11 rows of eight pieces each, creating diagonal rows of matching squares as

sandy
KLOP

Here's a tip to make sewing my quilt a piece of cake: Pretend you are just playing.

If I were in charge of the music for the carnival cakewalk, the song I'd play most is: "Bohemian Rhapsody" by Queen or Leonard Cohen's "Hallelujah."

When it comes to notions and tools, this one takes the cake for me: My Clover cutter embedded in an alphabet block. Mine is letter A. It was a gift from Moda.

Any way you slice it, the best thing about a Layer Cake is: It's so easy to slice up multiple layers.

Take a number. When buying fabric to use along with a Layer Cake: I use my ice cream pin dot because it goes with everything!

Food for thought: What's one thing you wish more quilters would do? I wish they would lighten up. And I love to see when quilters start with one of my patterns and make it their own.

What's the frosting on the cake for you in the quiltmaking process? I love it all! Selecting the fabric, cutting it up into little piles, sewing it together, the smells of a hot iron pressing, then the quilting and binding. "Look what I did!"

When slicing up a Layer Cake, my go-to ruler is: a 6½" × 12" ruler.

What is your go-to batting between quilt layers? Quilters Dream request weight.

My all-time favorite cake is: My mother made the best sunshine cake. It's light with multiple creamy layers!

AmericanJane.com

shown in the quilt assembly diagram. Sew the pieces into rows. Join the rows to complete the quilt top. The quilt top should measure 68½" × 94".

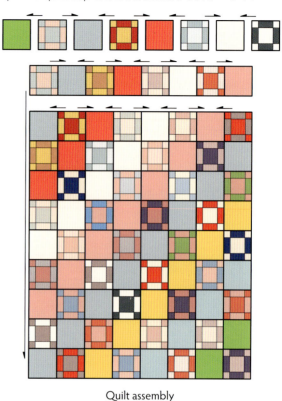

Quilt assembly

finishing the quilt

Find free, detailed finishing instructions online at ShopMartingale.com/HowtoQuilt.

1 Prepare the quilt backing so it's about 8" larger in both directions than the quilt top.

2 Layer the backing, batting, and quilt top. Baste the layers together.

3 Hand or machine quilt as desired. The quilt shown is machine quilted with parallel vertical lines.

4 Use the navy dot 2½"-wide strips to make binding. Attach the binding to the quilt.

churn it up

By LYNNE BOSTER HAGMEIER

Sometimes simple is best. Snowball blocks and sashing have added charm when combined with blocks in the border that create a secondary design of Churn Dashes. The tan prints sparkle when set against the dark prints to make a scrap-happy quilt.

FINISHED QUILT	FINISHED BLOCK
61½" × 61½"	7" × 7"

materials

Yardage is based on 42"-wide fabric.

28 squares, 10" × 10", of dark prints for blocks*
12 squares, 10" × 10", of tan prints for blocks*
2⅛ yards of green print for border blocks, border sashing, and binding
3⅞ yards of fabric for backing
68" × 68" piece of batting

A Moda Fabrics Layer Cake contains 42 squares, 10"×10". Lynne used the Kansas Troubles Quilters Milestones Layer Cake, which had only 11 tan squares, so she pulled an additional tan square from her stash.

cutting

All measurements include ¼"-wide seam allowances. Separate the dark 10" squares from the tan 10" squares. Refer to the cutting diagrams below to cut the dark 10" squares.

From *each* of 25 dark squares, cut:
1 square, 7½" × 7½" (25 total)
2 rectangles, 2½" × 7½" (50 total)

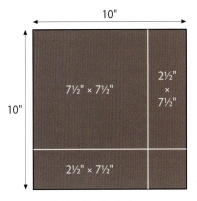

Cutting for 25 dark squares

From *each* of the 3 remaining dark squares, cut:
4 rectangles, 2½" × 7½" (12 total; 2 are extra)

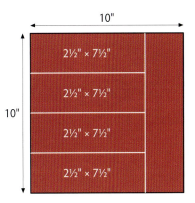

Cutting for 3 dark squares

Continued on page 47

Continued from page 45

From *each* of the 12 tan squares, cut:

4 strips, 2½" × 10"; crosscut into 16 squares,
2½" × 2½" (192 total; 12 are extra)

From the green print, cut:

5 strips, 7½" × 42"; crosscut into 24 squares,
7½" × 7½"

12 strips, 2½" × 42"; crosscut *5 of the strips*
into 24 rectangles, 2½" × 7½"

making the blocks

Press all seam allowances as indicated by the arrows.

1 Draw a diagonal line from corner to corner on
the wrong side of 144 tan squares. Layer a
marked square on each corner of a dark 7½" square,
right sides together. Sew on the marked lines. Trim
the excess corner fabric ¼" from the stitched lines.
Make 25 Snowball blocks measuring 7½" square,
including seam allowances.

 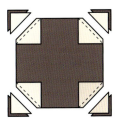

Snowball block.
Make 25 blocks,
7½" × 7½".

lynne
HAGMEIER

★

Here's a tip to make sewing my quilt a piece of cake: Use an accurate marking tool, like a chalk marker or sharp pencil for the connecting corners.

If I were in charge of the music for the carnival cakewalk, the song I'd play most is: "Girls Just Want to Have Fun" by Cyndi Lauper.

When it comes to notions and tools, this one takes the cake for me: I love the Quilters Select rotary cutter. It's heavier and feels balanced in your hand.

Any way you slice it, the best thing about Layer Cakes is: It's a good sampling of a fabric line.

Take a number. When I'm buying fabric to use along with a Layer Cake: I'll choose 1½ yards of a good tan for sashing and background and 2 yards of a coordinating dark for borders and binding.

Food for thought: What's one thing you wish more quilters would do? Use precuts; they're great for a scrappy quilt. Don't let the pinked edges scare you!

What's the frosting on the cake for you in the quiltmaking process? I love seeing my computer-generated design turn into a real quilt.

When slicing up a Layer Cake, my go-to ruler and rotary cutter are: Quilters Select 3" × 12" and 4½"-square rulers. The thin lines and nonslip back makes a huge difference when cutting and trimming.

There's always room for cake. True confessions—how many Layer Cakes are in your stash now? Too many of my own to count (at least one from each fabric collection). I have about a dozen other Moda designer's Layer Cakes for future projects.

Eat dessert first. What's your favorite treat before beginning a new project? I try to create a clean slate—leftovers from previous projects put away, design wall cleared, and a few bobbins wound. And an iced chai tea by my machine.

My all-time favorite cake is: My Mom's oatmeal cake with broiled coconut frosting. Yum!

ktquilts.com

By **LYNNE HAGMEIER**; pieced by **KATHY LIMPIC**;
quilted by **JOY JOHNSON**

2 In the same way, sew marked tan squares to two adjacent corners of a green 7½" square to make a border block. Make 20 blocks measuring 7½" square, including seam allowances.

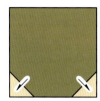

Border block.
Make 20 blocks,
7½" × 7½".

3 Sew a marked tan square to one corner of a green 7½" square to make a corner block. Make four blocks measuring 7½" square, including seam allowances.

Corner block.
Make 4 blocks,
7½" × 7½".

assembling the quilt top

Lay out the corner blocks, green rectangles, border blocks, remaining tan squares, dark rectangles, and Snowball blocks in 13 rows as shown in the quilt assembly diagram. Sew the pieces into rows. Join the rows to complete the quilt top. The quilt top should measure 61½" square.

finishing the quilt

Find free, detailed finishing instructions online at ShopMartingale.com/HowtoQuilt.

1 Prepare the quilt backing so it's about 6" larger in both directions than the quilt top.

2 Layer the backing, batting, and quilt top. Baste the layers together.

3 Hand or machine quilt as desired. The quilt shown is machine quilted with a feathered wreath in each block, Xs in the sashing squares, and parallel straight lines in the border.

4 Use the green 2½"-wide strips to make binding. Attach the binding to the quilt.

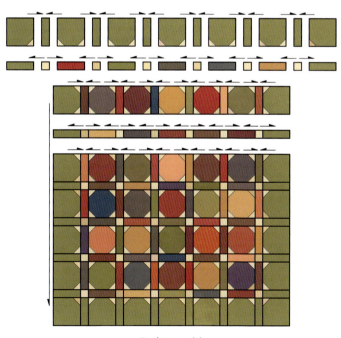

Quilt assembly

celebrate

By BARBARA GROVES and MARY JACOBSON

With so many ways to cut up Layer Cake squares, it's easy to make magical designs. In this delightful quilt the pieces come together to create twinkling stars. Stitch a flower motif in the white background and you'll be celebrating spring all year long.

FINISHED QUILT	FINISHED BLOCK
54½" × 64½"	10" × 10"

materials

Yardage is based on 42"-wide fabric.

30 squares, 10" × 10", of assorted prints for blocks and border*
2⅞ yards of white solid for blocks
⅝ yard of aqua print for binding
3½ yards of fabric for backing
61" × 71" piece of batting

A Moda Fabrics Layer Cake contains 42 squares, 10" × 10".

cutting

All measurements include ¼"-wide seam allowances. Refer to the cutting diagram below for cutting the assorted print 10" squares.

From each of the 30 assorted print squares, cut:
1 square, 4½" × 4½" (30 total)
4 squares, 3" × 3" (120 total)
1 strip, 2½" × 10" (30 total)

From the white solid, cut:
11 strips, 3½" × 42"; crosscut into 120 squares, 3½" × 3½"
10 strips, 3" × 42"; crosscut into 120 squares, 3" × 3"
15 strips, 1½" × 42"; crosscut into 120 rectangles, 1½" × 4½"

From the aqua print, cut:
7 strips, 2½" × 42"

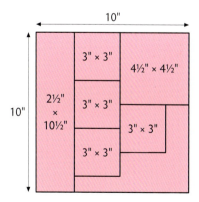

Cutting for 30 assorted print squares

By **BARBARA GROVES** and **MARY JACOBSON**;
quilted by **SHARON ELSBERRY**

making the blocks

Press all seam allowances as indicated by the arrows.

1 Mark a diagonal line from corner to corner on the wrong side of each white 3" square. Layer a marked square on a print 3" square, right sides together. Sew ¼" from both sides of the drawn line. Cut the unit apart on the marked line to make two half-square-triangle units. Trim the units to 2½" square, including seam allowances. Make 240 units, keeping like prints together.

Make 240 units.

2 Join two matching half-square-triangle units to make a flying-geese unit. Make 120 units measuring 2½" × 4½", including seam allowances.

Make 120 units,
2½" × 4½".

3 Sew a white 1½" × 4½" rectangle to the bottom edge of a flying-geese unit to make a side unit. Make 120 units measuring 3½" × 4½", including seam allowances.

Make 120 units,
3½" × 4½".

PRESSING MATTERS

Try using a curved pressing stick to press seam allowances open as you go. It will save time and trips to the ironing board. Once you finish your blocks, give them a good press with your steam iron.

4 Lay out four white 3½" squares, four side units, and one print 4½" square in three rows. The side units and 4½" square should be from the same print. Sew the pieces into rows. Join the rows to make a block. Make 30 blocks measuring 10½" square, including seam allowances.

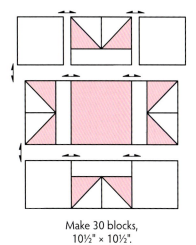

Make 30 blocks,
10½" × 10½".

assembling the quilt top

1 Lay out the blocks in six rows of five blocks each as shown in the quilt assembly diagram below. Sew the blocks into rows. Join the rows to make a quilt-top center measuring 50½" × 60½", including seam allowances.

2 Join the print 2½" × 10" strips end to end to make a long strip. From the pieced strip, cut two 54½"-long strips and two 60½"-long strips.

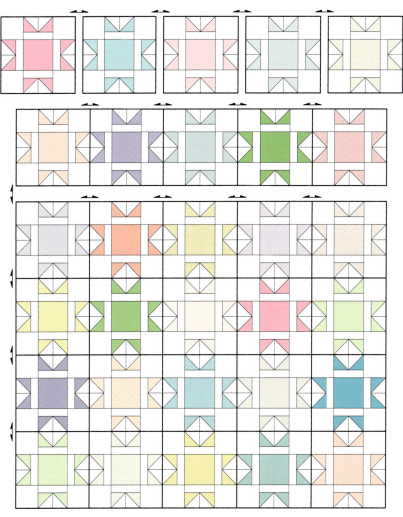

Quilt assembly

3 Sew the longer strips to opposite sides of the quilt-top center. Sew the shorter strips to the top and bottom to complete the quilt top. The quilt top should measure 54½" × 64½".

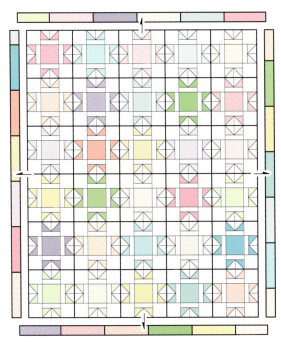

Adding the border

finishing the quilt

Find free, detailed finishing instructions online at ShopMartingale.com/HowtoQuilt.

1 Prepare the quilt backing so it's about 6" larger in both directions than the quilt top.

2 Layer the backing, batting, and quilt top. Baste the layers together.

3 Hand or machine quilt as desired. The quilt shown is machine quilted with a flower motif in the white area where each set of four blocks comes together, doubled curved lines in the center of each block, dense back-and-forth lines in the 1½"-wide strips in each block, and loops in the border.

4 Use the aqua 2½"-wide strips to make binding. Attach the binding to the quilt.

barbara
GROVES
and mary
JACOBSON

Here's a tip to make sewing our quilt a piece of cake: Press your seam allowances open. The blocks lay flatter and our long-arm quilter loves us for this!

If Mary were in charge of the music for the carnival cakewalk, the song she'd play most is: "Twist and Shout" sung by the Beatles.

When it comes to notions and tools, this one takes the cake for Barb: Still my favorite, the OLFA rotary cutter. Where would any of us be without it?

Any way you slice it, the best thing about a Layer Cake is: the frosting! We both love a good buttercream!

Take a number. When buying fabric to use along with a Layer Cake, Mary says: I buy three yards of something I love. It's enough for background or borders and maybe even a backing.

Food for thought: What's one thing you both wish more quilters would do? Don't stress! We've seen people in class fret over the smallest details, like which way the thread should twist when it comes off the spool! Who cares? Relax and have fun.

What's the frosting on the cake for Barb in the quiltmaking process? Hand sewing the binding.

When slicing up a Layer Cake, Mary's go-to ruler and rotary cutter are: my trusty 8½" × 12" ruler with worn markings and an OLFA 45 mm.

There's always room for cake. True confessions—how many Layer Cakes are in Barb's stash now? 426! I just counted. I'm making kits for a class. ☺

Eat dessert first. What's Barb's favorite treat before beginning a new project? Turn on the TV, tidy the sewing space, fill the iron, and get sewing!

What is Mary's go-to batting between quilt layers? Quilters Dream Poly Select. It's best for photography and it's lightweight for trunk shows.

Barb's favorite cake is: pineapple upside-down!

MeandMySisterDesigns.com

checkmate

By BRIGITTE HEITLAND

Let your fabrics flourish in an explosion of alternating colors! Checkmate is effortless to create using Layer Cake squares and strip piecing. With its trouble-free design and manageable size, this is an ideal project to whip up in a weekend.

FINISHED QUILT	FINISHED BLOCK
72½" × 72½"	8" × 8"

materials

Yardage is based on 42"-wide fabric.

81 squares, 10" × 10", of assorted prints for blocks*
⅝ yard of blue print for binding
4½ yards of fabric for backing
81" × 81" piece of batting

A Moda Fabrics Layer Cake contains 42 squares, 10" × 10".

cutting

All measurements include ¼"-wide seam allowances.

From *each* of the 81 assorted print squares, cut:
4 strips, 2½" × 10" (324 total)

From the blue print, cut:
8 strips, 2½" × 42"

making the blocks

Press all seam allowances as indicated by the arrows.

1 Using two strips from one print and two strips from a different print, join the strips along their long edges to make a strip set measuring 8½" × 10", including seam allowances. Make 81 strip sets. Cut each strip set into four segments, 2½" × 8½" (324 total). Note that you will use all of the strip set, so cut carefully.

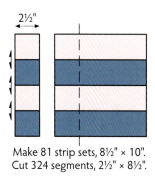

Make 81 strip sets, 8½" × 10".
Cut 324 segments, 2½" × 8½".

FABRIC FLEXIBILITY

If you experience a cutting mishap and need to substitute with a strip or two from your stash, don't worry. Fabric substitutions won't stand out in a quilt as scrappy as this and may even add to the appeal! Just match the value of the fabric you're replacing, and the overall look will remain consistent.

2 Lay out four matching segments from step 1, noting the orientation of the segments. Join the segments to make a block. Make 81 blocks measuring 8½" square, including seam allowances.

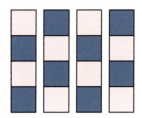 

Make 81 blocks,
8½" × 8½".

assembling the quilt top

Lay out the blocks in nine rows of nine blocks each, rotating the blocks as desired. Sew the blocks into rows. Join the rows to complete the quilt top. The quilt top should measure 72½" square.

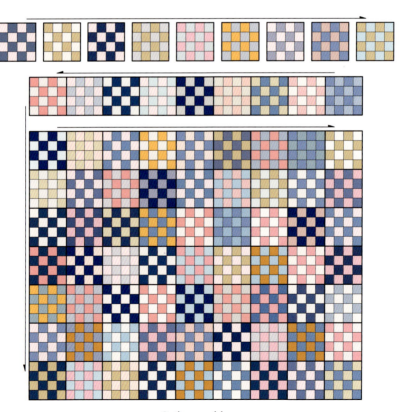

Quilt assembly

By **BRIGITTE HEITLAND;** pieced by **ALISON DALE;**
quilted by **CRYSTAL ZAGNOLI** of the Quilted Cricket

brigitte
HEITLAND

Here's a tip to make sewing my quilt a piece of cake: Prepare and cut in advance so you won't have to go back and forth to find all the cut pieces.

If I were in charge of the music for the carnival cakewalk, the song I'd play most is: "Happy" by Pharrell Williams.

When it comes to notions and tools, this one takes the cake for me: A Bloc Loc ruler for making half-square triangles perfectly.

Any way you slice it, the best thing about Layer Cakes is: the variety of a complete fabric collection on a lower budget.

Take a number. When buying fabric to use along with a Layer Cake: I get about three yards of a solid or a blender.

Food for thought: What's one thing you wish more quilters would do? Plan their fabric choices in advance based on where the quilt will be used.

What's the frosting on the cake for you in the quiltmaking process? To have the quilt on the long-arm machine and be stitching all the layers together.

When slicing up a Layer Cake, my go-to ruler and rotary cutter are: a 12½"-square ruler and a 60 mm rotary cutter.

There's always room for cake. True confessions—how many Layer Cakes are in your stash now? A lot. Since all my collections come with Layer Cakes and I work with them for new samples, I have at least one Layer Cake per fabric collection.

Eat dessert first. What's your favorite treat before beginning a new project? Download an audiobook and place a cool drink next to my sewing machine.

My all-time favorite cake is: *Apfelstrudel* from Vienna (my Granny is from Vienna).

BrigitteHeitland.de

finishing the quilt

Find free, detailed finishing instructions online at ShopMartingale.com/HowtoQuilt.

1 Prepare the quilt backing so it's about 8" larger in both directions than the quilt top.

2 Layer the backing, batting, and quilt top. Baste the layers together.

3 Hand or machine quilt as desired. The quilt shown is machine quilted with an allover swirl-and-feather design.

4 Use the blue 2½"-wide strips to make binding. Attach the binding to the quilt.

indigo aweigh

By LISA BONGEAN

Tiny Nine Patches march across the cream background to make this quilt a traditional favorite. The wide-open spaces give you (or a quilter you rely on) plenty of room for showing off gorgeous quilting designs.

FINISHED QUILT	FINISHED BLOCK
57" × 67½"	7½" × 7½"

materials

Yardage is based on 42"-wide fabric.

11 squares, 10" × 10", of cream prints for blocks and inner border*

16 squares, 10" × 10", of indigo prints for blocks and inner border*

4¼ yards of cream solid for blocks, setting squares, setting triangles, outer border, and binding

3½ yards of fabric for backing

63" × 74" piece of batting

A Moda Fabrics Layer Cake contains 42 squares, 10" × 10".

cutting

All measurements include ¼"-wide seam allowances.

From the assorted cream print squares, cut a *total* of:
88 strips, 1" × 10"

From the assorted indigo print squares, cut a *total* of:
140 strips, 1" × 10"

From the cream solid, cut:
2 strips, 13" × 42"; crosscut into:
    4 squares, 13" × 13"; cut the squares into quarters diagonally to yield 16 side triangles (2 are extra)
    2 squares, 8" × 8"; cut the squares in half diagonally to yield 4 corner triangles
3 strips, 8" × 42"; crosscut into 12 squares, 8" × 8"
6 strips, 6½" × 42"
7 strips, 2½" × 42"
15 strips, 2" × 42"; crosscut into:
    80 rectangles, 2" × 5"
    80 squares, 2" × 2"

making the blocks

Press all seam allowances as indicated by the arrows.

1 Join two indigo strips and one cream print strip to make a strip set measuring 2" × 10", including seam allowances. Make 40 of strip set A. Cut each strip set into nine 1" × 2" segments (360 total).

Make 40 A strip sets, 2" × 10".
Cut 360 segments, 1" × 2".

2 Join two cream print strips and one indigo strip to make a strip set measuring 2" × 10", including seam allowances. Make 20 of strip set B. Cut each strip set into nine 1" × 2" segments (180 total).

Make 20 B strip sets, 2" × 10".
Cut 180 segments, 1" × 2".

3 Join two A segments and one B segment to make a nine-patch unit. Make 180 units measuring 2" square, including seam allowances.

Make 180 units,
2" × 2".

4 Lay out five nine-patch units and four cream solid 2" squares in three rows of three. Sew the pieces into rows. Join the rows to make a double nine-patch unit. Make 20 units measuring 5" square, including seam allowances.

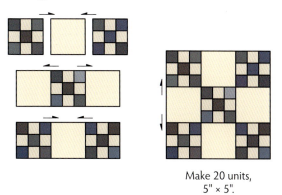

Make 20 units,
5" × 5".

5 Lay out four nine-patch units, four cream solid 2" × 5" rectangles, and one double-nine-patch unit in three rows of three. Sew the pieces into rows. Join the rows to make a block. Make 20 blocks measuring 8" square, including seam allowances.

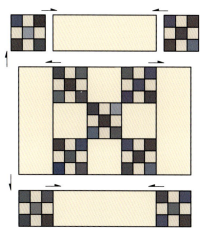

Make 20 blocks,
8" × 8".

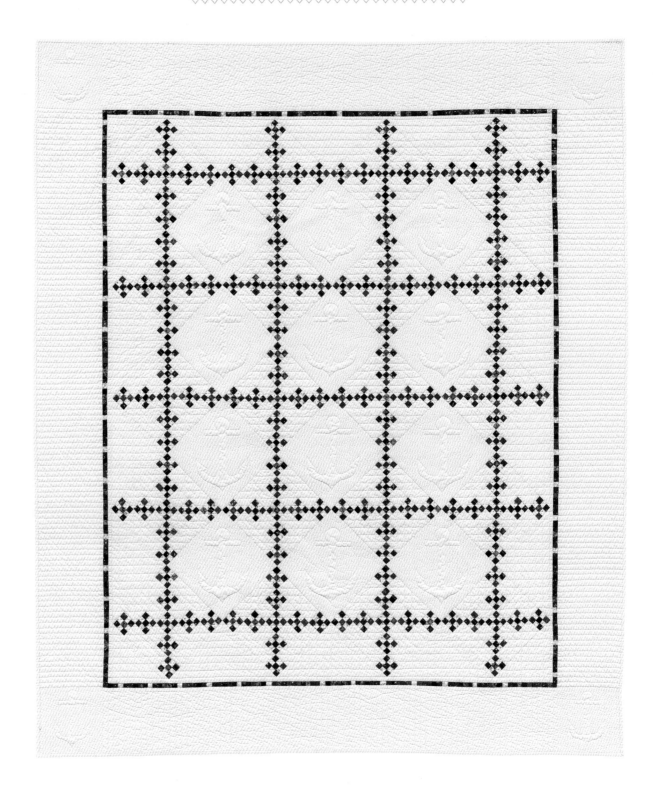

By **LISA BONGEAN**; quilted by **VALERIE KRUEGER**

making the inner border

1 Sew together 10 indigo and two cream print strips to make a strip set measuring 6½" × 10", including seam allowances. Make four of strip set C. Cut each strip set into nine segments, 1" × 6½" (36 total).

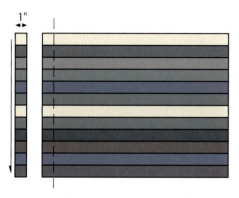

Make 4 C strip sets, 6½" × 10".
Cut 36 segments, 1" × 6½".

2 Join the C segments end to end to make one long strip. From the pieced strip, cut two 54½"-long strips for the side borders and two 45"-long strips for the top/bottom borders.

Side borders.
Make 2 borders, 1" × 54½".

Top/bottom borders.
Make 2 borders, 1" × 45".

assembling the quilt top

1 Lay out the blocks, cream 8" squares, and cream side and corner triangles in diagonal rows as shown in the quilt assembly diagram. Sew the pieces into rows. Join the rows, adding the corner triangles last, to make the quilt-top center.

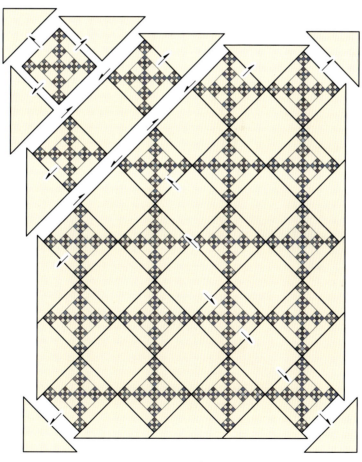

Quilt assembly

2 Trim and square up the quilt top, making sure to leave ¾" beyond the points of all blocks for seam allowances. The quilt top should measure 44" × 54½", including seam allowances.

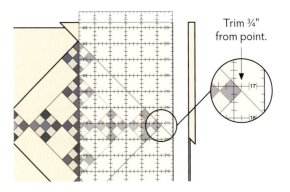

Trim ¾" from point.

3 Sew the 54½"-long inner-border strips to opposite sides of the quilt top. Sew the 45"-long inner-border strips to the top and bottom. The quilt top should measure 45" × 55½", including seam allowances.

PERSONALIZE YOUR QUILTING

Choose a quilting motif to personalize your quilts or carry out a theme. For instance, anchors are one of Lisa's favorite symbols. So she asked Val (her machine quilter) to quilt anchors in the alternate blocks. Val surrounded them with lots of background quilting to make them pop, like faux trapunto. When washed, the quilt not only has a vintage feel, but the quilting motif really stands out!

4 Join the cream solid 6½"-wide strips end to end to make a long strip. From the long strip, cut two 55½"-long strips and two 57"-long strips. Sew the 55½"-long strips to opposite sides of the quilt top. Sew the 57"-long strips to the top and bottom to complete the quilt top. The quilt top should measure 57" × 67½".

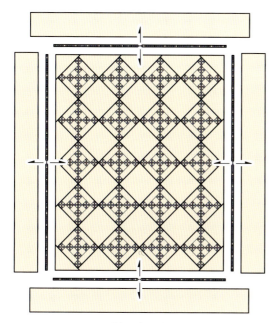

Adding borders

finishing the quilt

Find free, detailed finishing instructions online at ShopMartingale.com/HowtoQuilt.

1 Prepare the quilt backing so it's about 6" larger in both directions than the quilt top.

2 Layer the backing, batting, and quilt top. Baste the layers together.

3 Hand or machine quilt as desired. The quilt shown is machine quilted with an anchor motif in each setting square, surrounded by dense parallel lines. Crosshatched lines are quilted through the blocks and setting triangles. Parallel straight lines are quilted in the outer border.

4 Use the cream solid 2½"-wide strips to make binding. Attach the binding to the quilt.

lisa
BONGEAN

★

Here's a tip to make sewing my quilt a piece of cake: The Creative Grids Stripology Ruler works well because you'll cut the Layer Cake into 1"-wide strips.

If I were in charge of the music for the carnival cakewalk, the song I'd play most is: Journey's "Don't Stop Believin'."

When it comes to notions and tools, this one takes the cake for me: I use the Stripology ruler and starch the Layer Cake squares before cutting.

Any way you slice it, the best thing about Layer Cakes is: You can make so many projects from a Layer Cake without breaking the bank!

Take a number. When I'm buying fabric to use along with a Layer Cake: I look for a solid because I usually can use all the fabrics in the Layer Cake even if they're the same color as the solid.

Food for thought: What's one thing you wish more quilters would do? Have a positive attitude. If we ask for help nicely, other quilters are happy to help and offer advice, both in person or on social media.

What's the frosting on the cake for you in the quiltmaking process? I like the cake and the frosting! I love all aspects of quilting!

When slicing up a Layer Cake, my go-to ruler and rotary cutter are: My Primitive Gatherings Creative Grids 5" × 15" ruler; it features dashed lines, ⅛" markings, and a no-slip grip!

There's always room for cake. True confessions— how many Layer Cakes are in your stash now? Too many to count. (This is like asking me my age!)

What's your go-to batting between layers of your quilt top and backing? Trust your machine quilter— they know best!

My all-time favorite cake is: Whether it's a birthday or wedding or any other occasion, my go-to is white cake with white frosting!

LisaBongean.com

fruitcake

By BETSY CHUTCHIAN

Even if you're not a fan of the perennial holiday fruitcake, you're sure to love a Fruitcake quilt. Just like the Christmas treat, this design is packed with goodies and surrounded by a lovely caramel color. So skip the candied fruit and days of baking to make a Fruitcake that will be loved for years to come.

FINISHED QUILT	FINISHED BLOCK
82" × 82"	12" × 12"

materials

Yardage is based on 42"-wide fabric.

51 squares, 10" × 10", of assorted medium and dark prints (collectively referred to as "dark") for blocks, sashing, and border*

3¾ yards of cream floral for blocks, setting triangles, and border

¾ yard of brown print for binding

7½ yards of fabric for backing

90" × 90" piece of batting

A Moda Fabrics Layer Cake contains 42 squares, 10" × 10"

cutting

All measurements include ¼"-wide seam allowances. Select the medium and dark fabrics from the Layer Cakes and set aside the light prints for another project.

From each of the 51 assorted dark squares, cut:

2 strips, 4½" × 10"; crosscut into:
    1 square, 4½" × 4½" (51 total; 10 are extra)
    6 rectangles, 2½" × 4½" (306 total)

From the cream floral, cut:

2 strips, 18½" × 42"; crosscut into 4 squares, 18½" × 18½". Cut the squares into quarters diagonally to yield 16 side triangles.

6 strips, 8½" × 42"; crosscut into 24 squares, 8½" × 8½"

7 strips, 4½" × 42"; crosscut 4 of the strips into:
    1 strip, 4½" × 34"
    1 strip, 4½" × 27½"
    1 strip, 4½" × 23"
    1 strip, 4½" × 16½"
    1 strip, 4½" × 16"
    1 strip, 4½" × 10½"

2 squares, 4" × 4"; cut the squares in half diagonally to yield 4 corner triangles

From the brown print, cut:

9 strips, 2½" × 42"

making the blocks

Press all seam allowances as indicated by the arrows.

1 Join four different dark rectangles to make an A unit. Make 64 units measuring 4½" × 8½", including seam allowances.

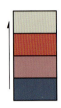

Unit A.
Make 64 units,
4½" × 8½".

2 Sew a dark square to an A unit to make a B unit. Make 40 units measuring 4½" × 12½", including seam allowances.

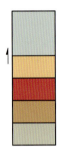

Unit B.
Make 40 units,
4½" × 12½".

3 Lay out one A unit, one B unit, and one cream 8½" square as shown. Sew the A unit to the cream square. Sew the B unit to the left edge of the square to make a block. Make 24 blocks measuring 12½" square, including seam allowances.

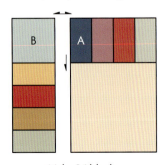

Make 24 blocks,
12½" × 12½".

making the border

1 Join the three remaining cream 4½"-wide strips end to end to make a long strip. From the pieced strip, cut one 4½" × 44" strip and one 4½" × 42½" strip.

2 Join 14 dark rectangles along their long edges. Sew the cream 4½" × 10½" strip to the left end and the cream 4½" × 44" strip to the right end of the strip of rectangles to make the top border. The border should measure 4½" × 82", including seam allowances.

Top border.
Make 1 border, 4½" × 82".

3 Join 12 dark rectangles along their long edges. Sew the cream 4½" × 42½" strip to the left end and the cream 4½" × 16" strip to the right end of the strip of rectangles to make the bottom border. The border should measure 4½" × 82", including seam allowances.

Bottom border.
Make 1 border, 4½" × 82".

4 Join 12 dark rectangles along their long edges. Make two. To make the left border, sew the cream 4½" × 16½" strip to the left end and the cream 4½" × 34" strip to the right end of one strip of rectangles. To make the right border, sew the cream 4½" × 27½" strip to the left end and the cream 4½" × 23" strip to the right end of the second strip of rectangles. Each border should measure 4½" × 74", including seam allowances.

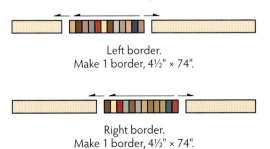

Left border.
Make 1 border, 4½" × 74".

Right border.
Make 1 border, 4½" × 74".

By **BETSY CHUTCHIAN**; quilted by **KAREN WOOD**

assembling the quilt top

1 Lay out the blocks, cream side and corner triangles, remaining B units, and remaining dark 4½" square in nine diagonal rows, noting the orientation of the blocks in the quilt assembly diagram below. Sew the pieces into rows. Join the rows, adding the corner triangles last to make the quilt-top center.

2 Trim and square up the quilt-top center, making sure to leave ¼" beyond the points

of the dark squares for seam allowances. The quilt top should measure 74" square, including seam allowances.

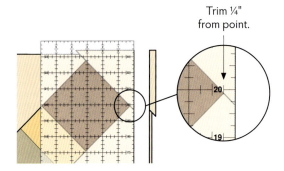

Trim ¼" from point.

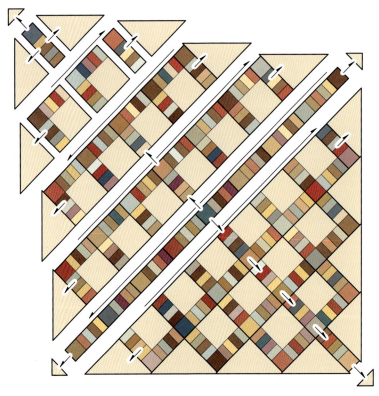

Quilt assembly

3 Sew the left and right borders to the sides of the quilt top. Sew the top and bottom borders to complete the quilt top. The quilt top should measure 82" square.

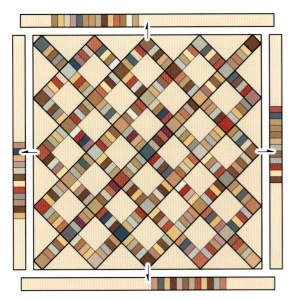

Adding the border

finishing the quilt

Find free, detailed finishing instructions online at ShopMartingale.com/HowtoQuilt.

1 Prepare the quilt backing so it's about 8" larger in both directions than the quilt top.

2 Layer the backing, batting, and quilt top. Baste the layers together.

3 Hand or machine quilt as desired. The quilt shown is machine quilted with an allover feather design.

4 Use the brown 2½"-wide strips to make binding. Attach the binding to the quilt.

betsy
CHUTCHIAN

Here's a tip to make sewing my quilt a piece of cake: Starch and press four Layer Cake squares at a time, then slice.

When it comes to notions and tools, this one takes the cake for me: OLFA Frosted Advantage Rulers for thin lines and accurate cutting.

Any way you slice it, the best thing about a Layer Cake is: the assortment of prints.

Take a number. When I'm buying fabric to use along with a Layer Cake: I generally get three yards of a companion print, which is usually enough for setting pieces or a border.

Food for thought: What's one thing you wish more quilters would do? Slow down and enjoy the process from fabric selection to cutting, sewing, quilting, and binding.

What's the frosting on the cake for you in the quiltmaking process? Choosing fabrics.

When slicing up a Layer Cake, my go-to ruler and rotary cutter are: a 6" × 12" OLFA Frosted Advantage Ruler and an OLFA Splash rotary cutter.

There's always room for cake. True confessions— how many Layer Cakes are in your stash now? At last count 10, I think.

Eat dessert first. What's your favorite treat before beginning a new project? I wish I had the discipline to clean up after a project, but I'm always so eager to begin a new one that I just shove things to the side and jump in.

What's your go-to batting between layers of your quilt top and backing? Whatever my long-arm quilter uses: 100% cotton or Hobbs Heirloom 80/20.

My all-time favorite cake is: Texas chocolate sheet cake or strawberry. It's a tie.

BetsysBestQuiltsandMore.blogspot.com

scissors happy

by KATHY SCHMITZ

What quilter doesn't enjoy a great pair of scissors? Express your love of scissors in a quilt that's super fun to piece. Choose a Layer Cake with neutral prints and add a touch of fusible appliqué to make a one-of-a-kind quilt.

FINISHED QUILT	FINISHED BLOCK
36½" × 36½"	8" × 8"

materials

Yardage is based on 42"-wide fabric.

20 squares, 10" × 10", of assorted light and medium prints for blocks and border*

12 squares, 10" × 10", of assorted dark prints for blocks, border, and appliqués*

1 square, 10" × 10", of light speckled print for border*

⅓ yard of black print for binding

2⅓ yards of fabric for backing**

41" × 41" piece of batting

1¼ yards of 18"-wide fusible web

Variegated cream/tan pearl cotton, size 12, or embroidery floss

16 buttons, ½" to ⅝" diameter

A Moda Fabrics Layer Cake contains 42 squares, 10"×10".

**If the fabric is wider than 41" after prewashing, you may need only 1¼ yards of backing.*

cutting

All measurements include ¼"-wide seam allowances. Set aside 6 of the darkest 10" squares for appliqué.

From *each* of 8 light or medium print squares, cut:
4 squares, 4½" × 4½" (32 total)

From *each* of 8 light or medium print squares, cut:
1 square, 8½" × 8½" (8 total)

From *each* of 4 light or medium print squares, cut:
4 rectangles, 2½" × 8½" (16 total)

From *each* of 6 dark print squares, cut:
16 squares, 2½" × 2½" (96 total)

From the light speckled print square, cut:
4 squares, 2½" × 2½"

From the black print, cut:
4 strips, 2½" × 42"

By **KATHY SCHMITZ**; quilted by **PAM PARVIN**

making the blocks

Press all seam allowances as indicated by the arrows.

1 Sew together four light or medium 4½" squares in two rows of two squares each. (In the featured quilt, two squares are from light prints and two are from medium prints.) Join the rows to make a four-patch unit. Make eight units measuring 8½" square, including seam allowances.

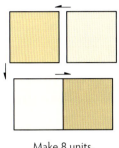

Make 8 units,
8½" × 8½".

2 Draw a diagonal line from corner to corner on the wrong side of each dark 2½" square. Place a marked square on each corner of a four-patch unit, right sides together. Sew on the marked lines. Trim the excess corner fabric ¼" from the stitched lines. Make eight Four Patch blocks.

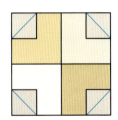
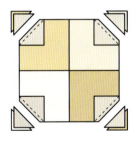

Four Patch block.
Make 8 blocks,
8½" × 8½".

3 Using light and medium 8½" squares instead of four-patch units, repeat step 2 to make eight Snowball blocks measuring 8½" square, including seam allowances.

Snowball block.
Make 8 blocks,
8½" × 8½".

4 In the same manner as in step 2, sew marked 2½" squares to the ends of a light or medium 2½" × 8½" rectangle. Make 16 border blocks.

Border block.
Make 16 blocks,
2½" × 8½".

5 Use the pattern on page 79 to trace 16 blades and 16 reversed blades onto the fusible web, leaving ½" between the shapes. Cut out the shapes, leaving about ¼" outside the drawn lines. Fuse the shapes to the wrong side of six dark 10" squares, following the manufacturer's instructions. Cut out the shapes on the drawn lines and peel away the paper backing.

6 Position a blade and a reversed blade on a Four Patch or Snowball block. Fuse in place.

Appliqué placement guide

7 Using one length of pearl cotton or six strands of embroidery floss, use various hand embroidery stitches to sew along the edges of the appliqués. (For embroidery stitch ideas, refer to the photo on page 76 and "Embroidery Stitches" on page 80.) Make eight of each block (16 total).

MIX IT UP, STITCH IT UP

Have fun embellishing all the scissors with a variety of stitches. Let yourself get carried away! After all, most of us quilters have more than one pair of beautiful scissors.

assembling the quilt top

Lay out the appliquéd blocks, border blocks, and light 2½" squares in six rows as shown in the quilt assembly diagram. Sew the pieces into rows. Join the rows to make a quilt top measuring 36½" square.

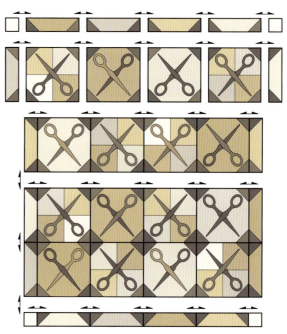

Quilt assembly

finishing the quilt

Find free, detailed finishing instructions online at ShopMartingale.com/HowtoQuilt.

1 Prepare the quilt backing so it's about 4" larger in both directions than the quilt top.

2 Layer the backing, batting, and quilt top. Baste the layers together.

3 Hand or machine quilt as desired. The quilt shown is machine quilted with an allover spiral-and-needle design.

4 After quilting, sew a button to the overlapping area of the blades on each block.

5 Use the black print 2½"-wide strips to make binding. Attach the binding to the quilt.

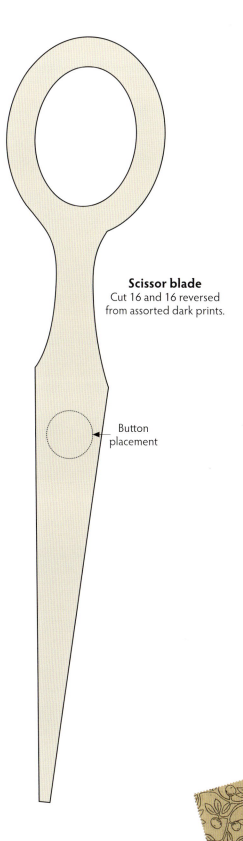

Scissor blade
Cut 16 and 16 reversed
from assorted dark prints.

Button
placement

 **kathy** SCHMITZ

Here's a tip to make sewing my quilt a piece of cake: Use lightweight fusible web. It makes the hand embroidery much more enjoyable.

If I were in charge of the music for the carnival cakewalk, the song I'd play most is: "Chicken Dance."

When it comes to notions and tools, this one takes the cake for me: KAI scissors! The micro-serrated scissors are perfect for cutting out appliqué pieces.

Any way you slice it, the best thing about Layer Cakes is: They're perfect for making an "intentional" scrappy quilt.

Take a number. When buying fabric to use along with a Layer Cake: I buy either a plain light or black fabric. I usually don't need to use yards and yards.

Food for thought: What's one thing you wish more quilters would do? Enjoy the journey! Every creative endeavor requires planning and preparation, so relax and enjoy each step.

What's the frosting on the cake for you in the quiltmaking process? If there is appliqué or embroidery, I'm in my happy place. I love tracing, cutting shapes, and stitching pretty stitches.

There's always room for cake. True confessions—how many Layer Cakes are in your stash now? I have five at the moment, but the quantity fluctuates.

Eat dessert first. What's your favorite treat before beginning a new project? Starting with an organized, clean space. Once I take the time to tidy up, I reward myself with hours of creative play!

What's your go-to batting between layers of your quilt top and backing? I like batting that's thin and limp, particularly wool batting because it doesn't hold the fold lines like some other batting fibers do.

My all-time favorite cake is: "It's a Winner" Chocolate Cake. Yep. That's what it's actually called.

KathySchmitz.com

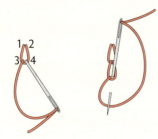

Chain stitch

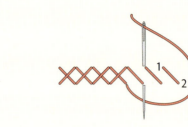

Cross-stitch

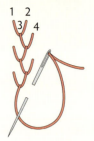

Feather stitch

French knot

Lazy daisy

Running stitch

Star stitch

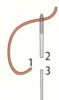

Stem stitch

Whipstitch